T0131623

Lindy
RECOVERING
ALPHA
FEMALE

**Inspiring Grace and Self Acceptance
in the Mind and Body**

LINDY LEWIS

BALBOA.
PRESS
A DIVISION OF HAY HOUSE

Cover graphics/art by Emerald Dumas

Balboa Press books may be ordered through booksellers or by contacting:

Balboa Press
A Division of Hay House
1663 Liberty Drive
Bloomington, IN 47403
www.balboapress.com
1 (877) 407-4847

Because of the dynamic nature of the Internet, any web addresses or
links contained in this book may have changed since publication and
may no longer be valid. The views expressed in this work are solely those
of the author and do not necessarily reflect the views of the publisher,
and the publisher hereby disclaims any responsibility for them.

The author of this book does not dispense medical advice or prescribe the use
of any technique as a form of treatment for physical, emotional, or medical
problems without the advice of a physician, either directly or indirectly. The
intent of the author is only to offer information of a general nature to help
you in your quest for emotional and spiritual well-being. In the event you use
any of the information in this book for yourself, which is your constitutional
right, the author and the publisher assume no responsibility for your actions.

Any people depicted in stock imagery provided by Thinkstock are models,
and such images are being used for illustrative purposes only.
Certain stock imagery © Thinkstock.

Print information available on the last page.

ISBN: 978-1-5043-3272-9 (sc)
ISBN: 978-1-5043-3273-6 (e)

Library of Congress Control Number: 2015907475

Balboa Press rev. date: 9/30/2015

"TO HEAR LINDY'S STORY IS LIKE READING A CHAPTER FROM THE LIFE OF ALMOST EVERY WOMAN I KNOW - SHE GIVES MEANING AND EMPOWERS US TO OVERCOME THE SEEMINGLY INSURMOUNTABLE OBSTACLES IN OUR PATH. I FEEL VALIDATED AND INSPIRED TO MOVE FORWARD WITH GRACE."

- Dr. Becky Meyer, fellow **RAF**
(**Recovering Alpha Female**)

WEBSTER NEEDS A FACELIFT!

LINDY'S LANGUAGE

500-Year Plan: Doing your personal best while you walk this planet with courage and the knowing that the impact will transpire over the next 7 generations.

RAF(Recovering Alpha Female): One who choses to soften and allow her beautiful feminine spirit to unfold, transform and inspire.

Ah-ha: Pivotal moment launching transformation.

Compassionist: One who holds a place of grace and compassion for self and others.

Feng Shui: Organization energetically

"Her": The woman who wants to live authentically, honestly and with more intention.

Hold Space: Patience and an honoring of your transformative process.

Humbling Blocks: Those moments in our climb that take us out of control and mess with our plan.

Let Your Color Out: Acknowledging and accepting one's quirks, then giving them expression.

Munay: Nourishing, all-encompassing love.

Perfect on Paper: Just that!

Processing Partner: That person you can be totally raw with and still feel loved.

Selfish: (A good word made bad) Learning to be more like yourself.

"They": Collective Consciousness; Society; them, everybody…family and friends.

Type A: An accomplished, over-achieving, accolade-driven, competitive, and ambitious personality.

Underground Kindness: (Lindy's non-profit) A quiet movement to bring balance to Public Education by presenting **Compassionists** in the classrooms, and introducing stress management tools, mindfulness techniques and unconditional acceptance to our **Youngers**.

Walk of Grace: That place of divine alignment where you accept all that is.

Woo-Woo: The crazy stuff, that works.

Woo-Woo Guru: Beautiful souls that choose (daily) to practice unconventional wisdom, energy management and trust in their knowing.

Youngers: These brilliant young people, our children, that teach us each day with their honesty, joy and living from the heart.

YOU-nique: Celebrating your authentic self, appreciating your true nature.

Zen Zone: That place of stillness we can go to when the noise of the world takes us out.

With great love and gratitude I thank the following 'colorful' souls in my life...

First of course, my own **Youngers** - Jerry, Cia and John - my children have witnessed and appreciate my transformation in to Grace. They teach and inspire me with their amazingly **you-nique** personalities!

My wonderful parents who blessed me with a loving and generous nature along with great compassion, Faith and confidence to tenaciously follow your dreams.

For my Omega, my man RHJ. His unwavering love, belief in my ability, and his unconditional love for me - such a gift in my life in so many ways.

For TAB, embracing and choosing the **RAF** Walk each difficult day. Showing me how important this work is and how powerful it can be when one with such little left on a material level can still embrace and nurture their remarkable spirit.

The Rainmaker team who has helped me bring my ginormous vision into manageable pieces in such a brilliant brand, and Emerald who designs the vision and has since joined **Let Your Color Out**.

A very special thank you to Lorna at Queen Bee for her writing, her dragon dictate deciphering, her uncanny knack for sassing, and collaborating to get this work into a book for my fellow Alpha's!

Lastly, my **Woo-Woo Guru's** you know who you are… you are my inspiration, my support and my strength in bringing this movement forward and to hold me so sweetly in this daily walk of recovery.

Thank you from my fullest most radiant heart.
Munay!!!

Lindy

WHAT LIES WITHIN

PROGRESS, NOT PERFECTION

IT'S NOT UNUSUAL FOR GOD TO WAKE ME UP AT 3 A.M. ON A REGULAR BASIS. In my Alpha Female days, I would get sooo irritated by this. After all, I needed to get up early the next day and get things done. Waking up in the middle of the night meant that I was not going to get the rest I needed, and so I would toss and turn in my frustrated state, trying in vain to fall back asleep. Instead, I would lay there and go over my checklist. The wheels would spin, and I'd find myself adding more and more items to it. As a **Recovering Alpha Female**, though, I've come to appreciate those 3 a.m. wakeup calls. God, the Universe, my highest self — whoever it is tapping me on the shoulder and whispering that I need to wake up now is really giving me the quiet time I need to hear my own intuition. So often, I find in the stillness of the night that there is some sort of thought flitting around that really deserves my attention and focus.

Now, when I wake up in the dark, I'm almost impatient to find out what it is. *What are you trying to tell me?* It may be necessary to take a breath and talk myself down so that I can have a little visit with God or whomever and hear my heart whisper. Lately, those wakeups have centered around how to share my journey with others so that they may embark on their own.

On one night in particular, awoken from my sleep, I stayed very still and waited for what would come. I had been constantly worrying about how best to communicate my story with others, and it seems that my subconscious had been working on the problem for me. The answer, and the generating force that led me to compiling these **ah-ha's**, came in the form of a story of how this all began.

WHEN I WAS A LITTLE GIRL, I would use fingernail polish to make signs on bark from trees. I would decorate them with words like "love," "peace," and "happy." Wanting to preserve these words and the wood beneath, I would cover them with clear nail polish. A little purple yarn was added so that the signs could be hung, and then I would gift them to my mom.

These were sweet gifts from a 10-year-old girl, to be sure, but I see that there was a deeper desire in giving the signs away. They were an outward, tangible manifestation of my loving nature. It felt important to me to give flowers and little painted signs to others to share the peace and love that I felt in my heart.

The signs were not just about self-expression; they were also a way for me to have that aspect of myself acknowledged by the outside world. Around this same age, I also began to condition the Alpha Female that I would become. The child who was so swept up in peace and love was still sweet and special, but these little projects were no longer an effective means of being recognized for the "right" things. These little pieces of art-and-soul didn't fit into the productive standard of our

THESE LITTLE PIECES OF ART-AND-SOUL DIDN'T FIT INTO THE PRODUCTIVE STANDARD OF OUR CULTURE.

culture. In fact, the very concept of trying to spread peace and love was counterproductive in a society that was always comparing us using a completely different measuring stick. The signs were cute, and the traits were admirable, but they weren't going to get me anywhere when it came to academia or the accumulation of the physical "stuff" that supposedly proves our worth and value.

Over time, the little girl that I was changed into someone else. As I determined that my dreams of peace and love weren't valued externally, I began to redefine my self-image. It became incredibly important to me to perform for others in order to get their approval and be deemed "worthy." Painting with nail polish and hanging messages of hope was replaced by getting a good spot on the volleyball team or winning ribbons on horseback or being one of the best water skiers around. These were the things that I thought others valued in me, instead of the loving, giving spirit that I learned to squelch.

It is only after engaging in the work I've described in this book, in discovering these **ah-ha's** for myself, that I have been able to come full circle back to that little girl who merely wanted to spread peace and love in the world. I had to buy wholeheartedly into the cliché and take a leap of faith. In doing so, I have been able to uncover my authentic self, and part of the essence of who I am leads me to want to help other women to uncover the aspects of themselves that years of distraction and "productivity" have buried. The best way that I know how to do this is to share my own stories that inspired and supported the journey of softening and awaking to my own inner beauty.

IT BECAME INCREDIBLY IMPORTANT TO ME TO PERFORM FOR OTHERS IN ORDER TO GET THEIR APPROVAL.

This has required my Alpha side and my Recovering side to collaborate, which has provided many lessons in itself. I have allowed the Alpha Female within to take the lead on things like collecting stories, setting deadlines, and doing the work to bring this to fruition. The Recovering side, however, has allowed me to step into this project with grace and humility. It has allowed me to forgive myself when things haven't always come together exactly as I pictured in my mind. The two sides are working together, even integrating themselves into a version of me who can be both soft and strong, both tough and feminine.

This is me living the idea of **"progress, not perfection."** This is me making mistakes but being OK enough to continue moving forward. Choosing progress over perfection has allowed me to do things like taking some time for myself. In the past, this made me feel incredibly guilty, because I felt that every moment should be devoted to my children, my job, my home, my community obligations, etc. I was constantly trying to make everything else perfect, and really preventing my own progress at the same time.

I NEEDED TO COME FULL CIRCLE BACK TO UNCOVER MY AUTHENTIC SELF.

The contradiction, of course, is that when I started taking time to know, honor, and listen to myself, I actually got better at other things. I became a better parent — one who could use a gentler tone and offer more grace to her children when they behaved like children. Not to be overly dramatic about it, but I really became more authentic. I walk more gently on this planet, I am more mindful of my own needs and how they relate to others, and I am carrying so much less anxiety and worry that would previously ripple out into the world around me and wreak havoc on my body.

PROGRESS, NOT PERFECTION.

Making the kind of progress needed to get reacquainted with your inner self — with your little girl who wanted to spread love or joy or whatever it was that fed your spirit — requires us to live in the moment. It requires us to listen to our hearts, rather than our heads. It takes time and patience to practice stillness, and for many of us, it also takes practice to come from a place of kindness rather than one of fear and anger.

Like life itself, this book is a journey; a daily practice. It is my journey, but my intention in sharing my heart is to provide others with the inspiration to make their own journeys fulfilling. I am not a guru who has spent years on a mountaintop seeking the wisdom of the universe. Instead, I am a modern woman who has learned how to open myself to accept the world and the differences among us and to **Hold Space** for myself and others to experience this existence in a way that is authentic.

MY DESIRE TO DO THE SO-CALLED RIGHT THINGS WAS ACTUALLY PREVENTING ME FROM DOING THE RIGHT THINGS.

I refer to myself, and others who choose to take this walk, as the **Recovering Alpha Female**. Like so many women, I used to focus all of my energy on today: having the "right" car, belonging to the "right" groups, being the "right" size, earning recognition for doing the "right" things, and having the title to prove it! I worked very hard to maintain this level, and I was highly successful at projecting the image of what I thought **"They"** thought I should be.

But, through an ongoing series of what I like to call **"Humbling Block,"** I began to recognize that my desire to do the so-called right things was actually preventing me from doing the RIGHT things. I now subscribe to the **500-Year Plan** — the idea that what I choose to do here and now can continue to have a positive effect on my children and my children's children, for generations to come.

I am owning my story. I have learned to manage my own stuff, and I claim both the good and the bad parts of it. By sharing how my tale unfolded, I hope to empower other Alpha Females to own theirs — to embrace your imperfections, your quirks, and the ways of thinking that make you **You-nique**. Your story will be your own, perhaps vastly different than mine, but my goal is to introduce some ideas that can be universally applied by those who are ready to step out of the shadows of who they "should" be in order to **radiate the light of who they truly are.**

THE ALPHA FEMALE DEFINED

THERE ARE MANY WAYS TO DETERMINE IF YOU ARE, IN FACT, AN ALPHA FEMALE. While some of the descriptors seem inherently negative, there are many, many positive aspects to the Alpha Female personality. For example, she is strong and charismatic. People tend to really enjoy her company and know that they are in good hands when she's involved in a project because she will lead it to success. The Alpha Female is often the center of attention with a gregarious personality, and her tenacity and perseverance are pretty much unrivaled. She is a visionary and is great at mustering her courage when needed. She is precisely the kind of outstanding employee, volunteer, family member, and leader that others hope for.

These are all great things, but there are down sides to being an Alpha Female. She continually measures herself according to someone else's ruler. She strives to gain external confirmation of her success, often becoming a work-aholic with unrealistic expectations for herself. And, when those impossible expectations aren't met, she becomes highly critical of herself. She tends to be overloaded in nearly every facet of her life, choosing to do so in order to feel like she is capable enough. But, there is a catch. No matter how hard we work or how many accomplishments and checks on the checklist we make, it will *never* be enough.

While the Alpha Female's life looks **perfect on paper** — she likely has a beautiful home, an impeccably kept yard with flowers popping up at just the right time, the kids dressed and spit-shined for the week's religious service, and a lively update in the perfectly-timed Christmas cards detailing her family's many achievements and travel over the previous year — looks are deceiving. While she appears to have everything in order on the outside, she

WHILE SHE APPEARS TO HAVE EVERYTHING IN ORDER ON THE OUTSIDE, SHE IS STRUGGLING WITH INTERNAL CONFLICT.

is struggling with internal conflict. She is constantly judging herself and coming up lacking. The attacking, critical internal narrative becomes a self-fulfilling prophecy and major stressor. The Alpha Female measures her self -worth based on accomplishments, accolades, productivity, and recognition from external sources. She is on a treadmill, running at full speed toward the next source of validation but never actually reaching a destination where she can stop and rest for a while or even take regular, healthy "breathers".

There is pride in being a driven person, in giving your best to what you choose to do. Unfortunately for the Alpha Female, however, she often doesn't recognize that she has a choice in what she does or thinks. Instead, she feels the need to do it all and expects the outcome to always be perfect. She is constantly striving for acceptance, to feel valued and appreciated, and so, often, her choices are made because she fears missing out on these things. Her head will easily override her heart's opinions and insights.

THIS IS MY DEFINITION OF THE ALPHA FEMALE. There may be others out there, but these are the words and traits I use. If you find that this depiction resonates with your soul, or that your spirit feels hopeful, then please read on, as this book was meant to find you. Join me in the journey to become a **Recovering Alpha Female**. It's not an easy process, no transformation ever is, but the freedom it will bring you is worth it. Working toward balance and what I like to call my Place of Grace can stir up a lot of uncomfortable feelings. In fact, part of the reason for the Alpha Female lifestyle is to remain too busy to have to acknowledge, let alone deal with, these often difficult and conflicting feelings in the first place.

When you boil it down, the Alpha Female bases her self-worth and acceptance on being valued by others. Whether she tries to gain it through external rewards and awards, by overworking herself for others' benefit in an attempt to prove her worth, or by relentlessly driving herself to perfection; she is all about gaining acceptance through productivity and contribution. She is all about "doing."

I am here to tell you that "being" is every bit as much a verb as "doing." Being is doing something. In fact, it's doing the most important thing of all. Being allows the truth and inspiration to come forward and make their rightful claim on you.

Hopefully by sharing my experience of living through this struggle can empower you to step forward honestly to actively participate in your own journey. What follows are my **ah-ha** moments and discoveries that were born from and contributed to my own transformation as a **Recovering Alpha Female**. I will do my best to support you as you move toward unconditional self-acceptance. I will **Hold Space** for your insecurities and feelings of separation when the path gets rocky and self-doubt dominates. And I will celebrate with you as you come to recognize the immeasurable intrinsic value of your own worth and wisdom.

INTRODUCING...HER

MAYBE THIS IS YOUR STARTING POINT IN THE JOURNEY OF A LIFETIME. MINE WAS NOT SO PRETTY:

It takes a lot to slow down an Alpha Female. But when it happens, it happens big. In my case being diagnosed with a serious autoimmune disease, Multiple Sclerosis, going through a bitter, angry divorce, and being thrust into a life of single-parenting three small children wasn't enough to do it. Nope. Despite these obstacles, I kept pushing myself harder. I found myself coaching soccer, volunteering in the classrooms, working more than full time. I was always trying to do more. Always trying to be more, to be enough…

Until I broke. I broke physically and I broke mentally.

"You look like shit."

Those words, spoken by me, about me, were the impetus for a transformative experience.

You see, life had become difficult. Really difficult. Normally, I was always on the go. There was work, and the house, and the kids, and a nonstop drive to be better. It all came to a screeching halt, however, when I herniated a disc as a result of pushing myself too hard, as if the disease wasn't enough. Of course, I had yet to realize that I had put myself in this position with my relentless desire to be and do everything. I thought I was striving to be more, but what I was really doing was trying to convince myself that I was enough.

Instead, I felt pitiful. My body was injured, and my spirit broken. Where I used to run, run, run, I could now barely advance at a crawl. For months I felt held back, lazy, and unproductive, spiraling further down into despair. There was no emergency shut-off, no valve to release the pressure to get back to my "happy" self and all of the obligations and accomplishments that entailed.

I THOUGHT I WAS STRIVING TO BE MORE, BUT WHAT I WAS REALLY DOING WAS TRYING TO CONVINCE MYSELF THAT I WAS ENOUGH.

Perhaps even more than pity, I felt a sense of self-loathing. I was always the person who could do it all, and here I was unable to do pretty much anything. I didn't realize how angry and disgusted I was until I caught sight of myself in the bathroom mirror one morning.

"You look like shit," I snarled at my reflection. I was tired, and I looked it. There had been no manicures, no painstaking application of makeup. I was worn down, and the sadness and confusion of my change in circumstance showed from the way I pursed my lips to the furrow in my brow. Then, I heard my voice again.

"Be nice to Her," I said.

And as I stepped into that third-person narrative, my compassion and empathy for the woman in the mirror began to blossom.

Here in these pages, I will **Hold Space** for you as you recognize the Her in your life and determine how to be nice to Her. I will support Her as she embarks on a journey of personal development and learns to trust Herself. I offer up the **ah-ha's** that played such an important part in accepting my own Her, becoming comfortable with Her, and even learning to celebrate Her. As you uncover your own Alpha Female tendencies and realize that you want something more authentic, you will find tools that can help in shedding beliefs that squelch the

> **AND AS I STEPPED INTO THAT THIRD-PERSON NARRATIVE, MY COMPASSION AND EMPATHY FOR THE WOMAN IN THE MIRROR BEGAN TO BLOSSOM.**

spirit — moving forward seeking a place of emotional stability and balance.

As we learn to offer kindness and unconditional acceptance to ourselves, it naturally ripples out into our homes, our families, and our communities so we can each make our own contribution to that **500-Year Plan**.

GO WITH YOUR GUT

I SPENT THE FIRST 40 YEARS OF MY LIFE DOING THE RIGHT THINGS. At least, I was doing all those things that everyone told me to do. My life was built on being great at meeting and exceeding their expectations. I stayed on track for all of the seemingly-important milestones that society had deemed were appropriate: I went to the right college to get the right major to get the best job. I married a man with the perfect resume, pedigree, and temperament. As I moved forward, I was continually working toward my fairytale future.

Frankly, I had a pretty fabulous life, according to the outside standards by which I measured that kind of thing. Everything looked beautiful, I was keeping it all together, and no one would have believed for a moment that I didn't have the whole fairytale thing locked in or the number of nights I cried myself to sleep feeling utterly alone. The trick, however, wasn't to fool them into believing it, it was fooling myself into buying the perfect-on-paper lifestyle.

There was this nagging voice within me that would occasionally pop up to say that something wasn't right.

I call it my "un-understandable" feeling, and it resided deep down in my core. On the rare occasions I would find myself consciously contemplating what this voice had to say, giving it perhaps more attention than was comfortable, my hyperactive mind would jump into overdrive and desperately throw water on what it knew could become a wildfire! And, with the next PTA meeting, work project, or perfect dinner party, I would narrowly escape having to acknowledge that the voice I was hearing was that of my heart.

When my heart would start its honest (yet scary) whispering, my brain would leap in to stop that voice. Whew! That was close! I didn't trust that voice. Or, more realistically, I was afraid that it spoke the truth. It took a very long time for me to recognize it for what it was — my own inner knowing. When one starts to accept that the heart whispers the truth, it likely means that change is on the horizon. And, let's be honest, change is scary. Especially when that change doesn't align with the fairytale or takes you in a completely different direction than what you've always been told is right.

What I realized is that in the first 40 years of my life, my mind was so active and beautifully creative in arguing its case that I was able to defend and justify my pragmatic thinking. My heart — my gut — didn't stand a chance. This awareness came slowly, with two pivotal life experiences culminating in ways that allowed me to finally see the truth. From all outward appearances, these experiences have little to nothing in common, but they were truly intertwined.

1. I said, "I do," when I had feelings of "I don't."
2. I was diagnosed with Multiple Sclerosis.

Often brides have a gut feeling that they should not be saying "I do" at that time with that person. Yes, my husband appeared to be everything a woman would want, but that little voice clearly tried to tell me otherwise. Instead of heeding it, I let my brain jump in and reverted to my default setting of trying to control everything around me. If force of will alone could have been enough, we would have had the ideal marriage. Instead, we ended up spending the next 12 years in a marriage that was loving, yet full of deception. It was a very lonely time, as there wasn't the kind of heart connection that is necessary for a strong marriage. Being the Alpha Female that I was, however, I was determined to fix it. I went into "doing" mode, and put considerable effort into trying to make my husband into what he appeared to be from the outside. The result was that we performed beautifully

THE RESULT WAS THAT WE PERFORMED BEAUTIFULLY AS A COUPLE IN PUBLIC, BUT THE INTIMACY AND TRUST JUST WERE NOT THERE BEHIND CLOSED DOORS.

as a couple in public, but the intimacy and trust just were not there behind closed doors.

We had gone to college together and developed a romance. Based on appearances, he was everything a young girl dreamed of. He was smart, handsome, and incredibly talented. He spoiled me with gifts. According to every external measure, he was absolutely top-notch husband material. And yet, there was a disconnect that my head couldn't fully understand. That little whisper would start up, trying to get me to examine the relationship. My inner knowing would pose questions, already recognizing

I WAS WILLING TO ATTEMPT TO CONTROL EVERYTHING AROUND ME TO GET MY FAIRYTALE FUTURE.

what the answers would be. It was trying to show me, to protect me, but I chose again and again not to place my trust in it.

When I would start to be hesitant, my mind would pipe in, making excuses and distracting me from the important underlying issues. I was already attached to the outcome I wanted — to that fairytale future, and I was willing to attempt to control everything around me to get it. This is something we Alpha Females have in common.

Why does this happen? Ultimately, it is a response to fear. I feared that voice and refused to give it credence. I couldn't trust it because I had never given it the opportunity to be right. Instead, I trusted my brain, which had shown me again and again that if I just micro-managed every detail, I would succeed in achieving what I wanted.

Don't get me wrong, there were truly beautiful aspects of our 15 years together, not the least of which is our three amazing children. As parents, we are supposed to be their guides in this life, but I now recognize that they play the role of the teacher.

The second experience where my gut was spot on, but I didn't want to know my knowing was when I realized there was something seriously wrong with me physically. Oddly, I knew I had Multiple Sclerosis long before I actually got the professional diagnosis. Not only did I have the symptoms moving around my body, but my instincts were telling me that it was MS. Who wants to validate that kind of knowing?

Not me — for sure!

SO, I RAN FROM IT. I kept myself from acknowledging it for ten years until I finally developed a foot drop, incredible fatigue, and a cognitive fog that started to seriously impede my life. I would forget to pick my children up at school or take them to their activities. When the diagnostic process proclaimed "Yes, you have MS," I really wasn't that surprised. My take-away from that experience was that it was the beginning of me recognizing how powerful intuition — the gut — really is.

I'm sharing these rather intimate aspects of my life because I suspect other women will see similar themes in their own lives. If you're so focused on living the dream that you are ignoring your own internal conflict, it's time to take a step back. What harm would come from taking some time to get centered and listen to your gut before making a big decision? If you suspect that you're making your choices — big or small — out of fear, consider that a red flag telling you that there is some important whispering going on, and you may have to work hard to quiet your mind enough to hear your heart.

Another word for these whispers is "intuition." **Your intuition is like a muscle,** in that the more you use it, the stronger it grows. The **Recovering Alpha Female** may have to start small, trusting only small bits of what her intuition is telling her. As its truth becomes more apparent, however, it gets easier to rely on your intuition. Over time, that little voice becomes a trusted best friend and a knowledgeable guide leading you through your beautiful life. And, as you trust your intuition more, you will find you don't really feel the need to seek advice from others or even care all that much about their opinions. Instead, you come to recognize and accept your own knowing.

"IT'S OK TO DO NOTHING." -RHJ

How do you hear that voice? First of all, it is imperative to quiet your mind and practice stillness. While you need to be physically active to strengthen your body, you need to be mentally still to strengthen your intuition. In my case, I took on the mantra **"It's OK to do nothing." -RHJ** I began to replace my fear with faith.

As you honor your own inner knowing, you find that conflict and resistance begin to fall away. You become truly strong and confident, as opposed to the false bravado that is so often the case when we're basing our value on accolades and achievements, while simultaneously trying to control our environment.

Remember that tomorrow has not been promised to any of us, so why spend so much time attached to an outcome that may or may not be there? Instead, lead with your heart and follow your intuition. Go with your gut, and don't worry so much about the fallout. In the words of Eleanor Roosevelt, "A woman is like a tea bag — you can't tell how strong she is until you put her in hot water."

Redesigning how you interpret and interact with the world can be a whole lot of fun, and is incredibly liberating. Just remember to love yourself through the process!

WOO-WOO
IS NOT COO-COO
Woo-Woo: The crazy stuff
that works!

**IF THE PREVIOUS SECTIONS OF THIS BOOK
HAVE RESONATED WITH YOU, THEN READ
ON WITH AN OPEN MIND.** My biggest hope is
that other women will also have those **ah-ha** moments
that allow them to offer themselves some grace. If
you've been reading along and nodding, or at least not
closing the book, then it's likely that you're ready to
start accepting yourself and to listen to your gut. So far,
I've not said anything that is too out there.

At this point my former Alpha Female side would bristle
and laugh at the things I'm about to share with you.
I would have called you a hippie or an earth mama or
possibly even a freak. After all, I was rockin' my life just
fine, wasn't I? I had all the kudos, accomplishments,
achievements, and stuff to prove it!

Then there was that MS diagnosis. I was terrified by the
progression the disease often takes. I might lose
mobility or bladder function or even my cognitive

abilities. On top of that, I had just recently added "single" as a prefix to "mother of three." I was scared and willing to do whatever the doctors told me to do. Each week I would inject myself according to the doctors' protocol, and I would feel incredibly sick afterward. I felt like I had to put my discomfort out of my mind and ended up bullying myself over thoughts that I needed to

THE BODY AND MIND ARE INTERCONNECTED, SO CARING FOR ONE HAS A POSITIVE EFFECT ON THE OTHER.

be at work more, keep the house up, and be a better soccer coach. I needed to bring home the bacon and make sure the kids didn't miss a beat.

How I treat my disease has changed quite a bit since that time nearly ten years ago. Since then, I have learned that the body and mind are interconnected, so caring for one has a positive effect on the other. For the last five years, I have approached the management of my MS with a combination of Western medicine and alternative therapies. These alternatives are what I refer to as **Woo-Woo**.

There was a time not too long ago when massage therapy was considered by many to be a bit coo-coo. Now, of course, we know that there are huge benefits to massage. Even your Western-educated doctor might prescribe that you get a massage for everything from an injury to stress. There are other practices that have been considered coo-coo or New-Agey that are gaining more acceptance.

I'll admit that I'm one of the people who was skeptical about these things. Chiropractic? Acupuncture? Aromatherapy? Even those more mainstream alternative healing arts still sounded pretty cheesy. There was no way that this Alpha Female was buying into the idea that something so far out of my own control could be effective. Taking a pill? Sure, I could get behind the science of medical treatment to keep me healthy. But… a karmic session or a Shaman taking you on a journey through the underworld? Yeah, not so much!

Until I tried it, that is. I actually agreed to a karmic session, completely sure that it was just a silly little thing to do and wouldn't have any real effect on my life. The practitioner closed her eyes and started "spinning the wire." She proceeded to tell me a blocked story from my life in the year 1368. Supposedly, this experience I had in a previous life was blocking me from being my highest self now. According to her, she went ahead and cleared the block.

Blah, blah, blah. This lady was clearly a FREAK. Really, who does that?

Humoring her, I asked what I needed to do to follow up. What kind of work was necessary for me to clear this block and shift my perspective? "It's done," she said. "You don't have to do anything." *Sure thing,* I thought, bidding her farewell and a special day in la-la land. I couldn't get out of there fast enough.

But, by the time I got to the car, I found myself giving it some thought. The story challenged my religious beliefs, for sure. If nothing else, it was definitely well into the **Woo-Woo** category. And, everyone knows that **Woo-Woo** is coo-coo, right? I happen to be tenacious, as is any true Alpha Female, so I forced myself to take a moment to just sit without judging the process or the totally irrational story. What I found was that I *did* feel different. I felt a sense of relief — a sense of peace.

I don't exactly claim to know how energy healing works, which is why the title of this **ah-ha** includes the somewhat derogatory term "**Woo-Woo**." That said, I strongly encourage other **Recovering Alpha Females** to give it a chance. This might require you to step pretty far out of your comfort

THE BODY, AND NATURE AT LARGE, WAS DESIGNED TO TAKE CARE OF ITSELF.

zone. It can be extremely difficult for those of us who want to be in charge to accept that which cannot be touched or thoroughly explained. Doing this kind of work means opening your mind to something new and moving forward without judgment. The key to this is suspending your judgment and going in with no expectations. You don't necessarily have to believe it's going to work, but take in the information with the idea that it could *possibly* work. Just being curious enough to check it out could be the very thing that helps shift some painful belief that you've been holding onto about yourself.

When I went to that energy healer, I spent the entire time unable to figure out how something like that could possibly work. Finally, I just said, "So what." So what if it's not real? Was there something I could still learn or gain from the experience? If nothing else, it might be a funny story to tell later.

SO WHAT? SO WHAT IF IT'S NOT REAL? THERE'S ALWAYS SOMETHING TO LEARN FROM THE EXPERIENCE.

The results of the sessions were so unexpected that I found myself pretty intrigued by this **Woo-Woo** stuff. I spent the next 18 months on a journey learning to do this type of energy work myself. The energy healer I met that day became one of my **"Woo-Woo Gurus,"** and my children participated as I learned the needed skills to do the work.

YEP, I JUST WENT FULL WOO-WOO ON YOU, DIDN'T I? Don't worry, I'm well aware that there is zero logic to it. I cannot reason or rationalize it or logic it out. What I can do, though, is see it work in my life and ripple out into others'. Through this work, I have been able to lighten my emotional and mental load to the point where I am finally able to not just accept, but even appreciate, the parts of me that used to cause me dread. For example, I've come to embrace my ADHD mind and the curves of my body that used to cause embarrassment.

For five years now, I have undergone a monthly intravenous treatment for my MS instead of weekly injections. This helps to slow the progression of the disease. Chiropractic, yoga, massage, acupuncture, energy work, and nutrition also play a large role in my care. I have integrated Western science-minded thinking with various **Woo-Woo** healing modalities, and as I have, I've been able to embrace the process of not only physical, but also mental change.

The fact that these alternative treatments are becoming more mainstream is a good thing for me. When I first started integrating them into my healthcare, there was resistance from medical providers, and resentment on my part because I had to pay for everything out-of-pocket. Insurance didn't cover them, and they were downright expensive. But, I would go to the healers and find relief. They empowered the physician within me while looking at my overall well-being, rather than just managing the disease.

It took me quite some time to really justify the expense to myself. I had to fight the idea that I was wasting my money on this **Woo-Woo** stuff. But, as I began to see improvements physically, mentally, and emotionally, it was hard to deny that it was worthwhile. I was actually starting to feel good. Maybe my **Type A**, Alpha Female couldn't see or hear or taste what was going on, but I'll be damned if I couldn't feel it. I was transforming. I began to celebrate the wonders of the mind, body, and spirit.

I BEGAN TO SEE THE IMPROVEMENTS PHYSICALLY, MENTALLY, AND EMOTIONALLY.

The body, and nature at large, was designed to take care of itself. Our eyes blink without effort on our part. Our colon eliminates toxins without our intervention. We do not have to focus our attention to breathe. Nature takes care of these things. It's not impractical to think that it takes care of far more than we realize.

Another reason that I had to justify these practices was because they tested my religious beliefs. I grew up in a strictly religious family and even attended a religious college. I always had an enormous amount of faith in God. Working with energy and recognizing that my body was a self-healing organism challenged my beliefs. At times, I worried that what I was doing could be considered witchcraft or paganism. What I ultimately found was that I was using that as an excuse. Really, my resistance came from the fact that things such as meditation, allowing myself to do nothing, and feeling my experiences was challenging my Alpha Female tendencies. Sitting and listening was counterintuitive to my "gotta be doing something" personality.

SITTING AND LISTENING WAS COUTERINTUITIVE TO MY "GOTTA BE DOING SOMETHING" PERSONALITY.

The medicine wheel, energy work, delving into the chakras — these were all foreign concepts that my mind tried to fight and figure... I didn't understand it. It wasn't something that I could logic out or even speak clearly about. I put a lot of time into studying these modalities, to try and make the ideas bend to my will, but when all was said and done, I had to forego some of my guarded control in order to simply accept that it was working. This blurring of my lines between black and white helped to soften my outlook on the world and myself, becoming a major point in my metamorphosis. I would strongly suggest keeping this to yourself in the beginning to avoid judgment that would reignite the self-doubt or belief you have just worked through.

Is this something that you could do? Could you open your mind to the idea that there is something much greater than our own understanding? If so, you may be able to experience the same type of softening I did in order to discover your own **Place of Grace or Zen Zone.** Softening, allowing, surrendering — these are all such feminine words that the Alpha Female fights. But life can be different, and even better, when we give up the illusion of control and release the fears that naturally come from being attached to our expectations. Detaching from the outcome of how things "should" be is an incredible method for experiencing peace.

I HAD TO FOREGO SOME OF MY GUARDED CONTROL IN ORDER TO SIMPLY ACCEPT THAT IT WAS WORKING.

WHO ARE "THEY" ANYWAY

AH, THE GOOD LIFE. I HAD IT, RIGHT? A beautiful wedding, an accomplished husband, three perfect children (both genders, of course), the right car, the house on the hill, traveling to all the right places… and, let's not overlook the great job where everyone thought I was awesome and I was making lots of money to go shopping and buy all the right shoes and handbags. I had it all!

I was also scheduled up to my eyeballs. I was keeping track of RSVP's to parties and setting more and more milestones for myself. If I had any uncomfortable feelings, I would quickly squelch them and look for some sort of external sign of accomplishment. I overloaded myself and subsisted on crumbs of kudos and "atta girls" from those around me. I kept myself distracted and rather successfully caught up in 'the race.'

I would achieve one set of goals, only to find a new set facing me. No matter how hard I tried, perfect just never came. In the meantime, I was building my façade so successfully that I began to lose my true identity. My days and nights were spent putting all my energy toward everyone else's needs. From the outside, I looked like I had it all dialed in, but when I was alone in the wee, dark hours of the night, conflict was abundant. I might be lying in bed next to my husband or one of our children, but I felt hopelessly lonely.

If I found myself with a quiet moment, unrest and conflict would surge within me. Of course, the Alpha Female can't stand that. There is no room for reflection and introspection in the life of a woman who is focused on putting out fires, managing deadlines, and attempting to be the perfect parent. Add to that the pursuit of physical beauty — the intolerance for the slightest bit of curvaceousness — and you have a peek into my "no pain, no gain" perspective at that time.

Keeping myself frenetically busy allowed no time for introspection. There was no opportunity to examine my life and find any unrest within it. This is the paradox for the Alpha Female. We have spent so much time running, running, running in an effort to be good-enough that we can't take the time necessary to be still and recognize that we already are! Time is a crucial component in connecting with our brilliant intuition. We must be meditative and **open to nothingness** in order to see how much we really have.

The process of slowing down is counterintuitive and uncomfortable at first. I would go so far as to say that it even feels unsatisfactory in the beginning. It's hard to sit and be quiet when you feel like you should be doing a million other things. And, the nagging feeling that you should be doing something else is only part of the discomfort, because being still gives those hidden thoughts a chance to come out of the shadows and make themselves known. Self-doubts make an appearance and try to drown out the authentic voice that wants so desperately to be heard.

WHEN YOU SURRENDER THE NEED TO BE AND DO IT ALL, THE JOURNEY OF UNCONDITIONAL SELF-ACCEPTANCE CAN BEGIN IN EARNEST.

This voice, while it is timid and sometimes afraid to speak up, is infinitely patient. It doesn't scream, but sits waiting for you to hear it. It offers gentle reminders to your heart. If it's overlooked for too long, though, it can manifest itself in physical illness as a way of forcing you to slow down and listen. This is what happened in my case. When you do quiet yourself, however, when you surrender the need to be and do it all, the journey of unconditional self-acceptance can begin in earnest.

Taking that first step into self-discovery is incredibly empowering, yet equally as vulnerable as you leave the shore of collective consciousness - the **They's** in your life. In choosing to develop your spiritual self-esteem and intimacy, you will learn to stand strong and even to enjoy the ongoing transformation that follows. You will become a part of the beautiful group of **Recovering Alpha Females** who have decided to live their best lives, rather than always focusing on what **They** say is right.

Who are **They**, anyway? "Well, **They** say that children should watch no more than 30 minutes of television a day." "**They** will think I'm fat." "**They** won't like me." Close cousins to **They** is *Everybody*. "*Everybody* thinks I should go." "*Everybody* says that a modern woman should be able to manage a home and a job." The ongoing quest to do everything "right" ends up polluting our own thinking and leaves us second-guessing ourselves. "What will **They** say?" "What will *Everybody* think?"

HAVING TAKEN THIS JOURNEY, I'VE LEARNED THAT "THEY" ARE A BUNCH OF LIARS AND HYPOCRITES.

Who the hell are **They** and *Everybody*, and why do **They** have anything at all to say about YOUR size or where you should go? Why should **They** get to determine what is true and correct for others? Why do **They** get to dictate what you "should" do?

The same thing applies to the old adage of "keeping up with the Joneses." Why on earth would you want to live the Joneses' life instead of your own? And just who are the Joneses trying to keep up with? My guess is that those fictitious neighbors are also caught up in the illusion of trying to do what **They** say!

Having taken this journey of self discovery, I've learned that **They** are a bunch of liars and hypocrites! I know this because I have backslid on living true to my authentic self, and I've seen the results. At times, I have reverted to my old patterns — to living life the way **They** say I should. What I found was that I don't really fit that mold anymore, and my life is far brighter for it. I have made friends with my inner voice. I listen to my intuition. And I am so much more fulfilled than I ever was trying to toe the line that **They** arbitrarily placed in front of me.

Still, I suspect I will continue to backslide or relapse often, and that's OK, too. Each time it happens that I try to fit back into that previous life, it illuminates my feelings of not

WHY DO THEY GET TO DICTATE WHAT YOU SHOULD DO?

belonging, of being separate or not enough. Sometimes I doubt myself because I haven't found my ultimate joy and passion on my journey. But, when I revert to those old ways of doing things, I recognize how much less fulfilling that lifestyle is. At this point, I have a foot in both camps as I continue to move forward. It can be a scary place to stand, teetering between the old and the new; but just as I **Hold Space** for your transformation, I also hold it for my own.

It may be hard to see at first, but it's worthwhile to put the effort in to recognize when **They** are making demands of you — when you're doing for *Everybody* instead of for yourself. A good way to start this practice is to define for yourself who **They** are. When you find yourself thinking, "Yeah, but *Everybody* says…" ask who this elusive *Everybody* is. I would even suggest you go so far as to write it down. The next time you start to go down that road of insecurity and judgment, when you feel self-doubt creeping in — you can turn to this list and uncover whether maybe you're actually responding to what **They** say instead of what is truly best for you.

Don't be surprised if this leads to one of those 'ah-ha moments' we hear so much about. If you find that you're having a hard time letting go of the conclusions and judgments that you're sure **They** are making about you, it might be time to dig a little deeper to shift your thinking. In my case, the **Woo-Woo** stuff played an important role in this. The energy work I've done was very powerful in helping me shed the beliefs that didn't serve me and helped me discover my authentic expression.

My spiritual muscles have been flexed, and I continue to strengthen them. Those doubts that come creeping in are one of the **humbling blocks** along my path that sometimes make me falter. But because I have *consciously* chosen to shift my attention away from what

They say I should do, I am so much better equipped to listen to my inner voice, to go with my gut.

As you start to experience the liberation of your spirit and mental freedom in your own Walk with Grace, keep in mind one of my favorite mantras: "A tiger doesn't lose sleep over the opinions of sheep." When it comes right down to it, ask yourself, "Who are **They** anyway?" Don't let them have your power!

GET OUT OF YOUR OWN WAY

IT'S TEMPTING TO THINK THAT ALL OUR PROBLEMS STEM FROM DOING WHAT THEY SAY WE SHOULD, but the truth is that we cause a decent amount of our own strife, too. As I said before, I sometimes falter on my own journey and go back to old patterns. I find myself with a little too much thinking time, and the next thing you know, I'm standing in front of the pantry. I eat sweet, I eat salty, I gnaw at my nails. When my Walk with Grace gets a little too real, and uncomfortable thoughts spring up in my stillness, I can find all manner of ways of busying myself. I organize the house, sweep the floor, scrub the countertops, play with the dog.

I'm not saying that cleaning or playing with the pooch aren't good things. Even sneaking a treat from the pantry once in a while has its benefits. But, when they start to take over, it's because that Alpha Female is trying to cover something up. I'm falling back into the pattern of constantly needing to see results in order to feel validated.

My desire is not to dishonor the Alpha Female within. She has served me well. She has done so much and rightfully earned accolades. She has rocked my world, and I trust her. The new challenge, though, is to allow things to unfold naturally, rather than to try to force them into being. Remember that **"being" is every bit as much a verb as "doing!"** So, I must move forward into a more grounded and centered place while also offering gentle kindness and respect to the Alpha Female that resides within me.

The **Recovering Alpha Female** is important, too. She is who I am becoming, and who I hope to inspire you to uncover in your own life. She is soft and gentle. She is empathic and compassionate. Above all,

THE RECOVERING ALPHA FEMALE NEEDS TO GET OUT OF HER OWN WAY AND MAKE PEACE WITH THE TWO ASPECTS OF HERSELF.

though, she honors herself. She gives herself the love that she deserves, and as a result, it ripples out through her interactions with others.

In order to get out of your own way, these two aspects of oneself must make peace with each other. The Alpha Female is a powerhouse, bulldozing wherever she goes and getting results. This is a great gift, but it also inhibits her. She needs to rest, to take a step back for her own good. That doesn't mean that she shouldn't be respected and appreciated for the strength and protection she has offered for so long.

The **Recovering Alpha Female (RAF)** is gentle and understanding. She is apt to take a backseat and allow the Alpha to run chaotically all over her. It's important to notice when this happens in order to get things back into alignment. For me, I might recognize this as I stand in front of the pantry, biting my fingernails and mentally building a to-do list of little things that supposedly need to be done. It is in these moments that I must remember that the **RAF** is even more powerful than her counterpart. I need to allow her to step forward and take the lead in her own loving, graceful way.

The two are one another's Yin and Yang, opposite yet complimentary sides of a coin. Each has her own talents and skills and purpose in this life. At this point, the Alpha Female has more than done her job. She may be called upon when needed, but it is the **RAF**'s turn to shine. It is time to trust her wisdom and knowing and to allow the Alpha Female to rest so she will be at her best when her skill set is called on.

It's amazing how, when you are approaching this realization, it can feel like the world is orchestrating to stop it. You may feel like you're standing on one side of a porthole that will take you to a whole new world, but there is something physically holding you back. As you approach breakthroughs, preparing to leap through that porthole, you may find that you feel tired, edgy, maybe even a bit lethargic. And, when you feel like that, there's nothing quite as comforting as reverting to the familiar in the form of old patterns. There you are, standing at the pantry making your way from sweet to salty and throwing in a milk chaser. You *know* full well that you are physically sabotaging yourself, and yet you feel a reluctance to do anything about it.

The physical sabotage moves to a mental level. "Look! You can't even stop yourself from binging on chocolate and pretzels, so obviously you can't move yourself to a higher level of consciousness. Step away from that porthole, loser, you don't deserve knowledge and inner peace; and you're not good enough to inspire and create the life you want!"

MY INNER KNOWING IS STRONG AND SMART, AND IT TELLS ME THAT I DON'T HAVE TO BE PERFECT.

This is a huge **humbling block** for me. My mind bullies me, tells me that I can't possibly encourage others to start their own journeys because I'm not perfect at my own. It is estimated that we average 60,000 thoughts each day (about 1 thought per second), and it is amazing how most of them can be self-defeating.

Fortunately, I've been doing this long enough to know that I need to get out of my own way. My inner knowing is powerful and wise, and it tells me that I don't have to be perfect. When these feelings rear their heads, it's time for me to look in the mirror and reassure Her that she is doing just fine. These words will reach those who are ready to hear them. It is not within my power to control who appreciates and accepts them. Instead, it is my place to release them into the world and let the Universe take care of the rest.

FIND SOMEONE AS NORMAL AS YOU

LET'S ASSUME THAT YOU HAVE MADE THE DECISION TO START RECLAIMING YOUR POWER. You are ready to bring your authentic voice forward. You have likely made peace with this decision, or are at least working toward that end, but others may not be so easily convinced.

When you start to hear and speak your own truth, you may find that you naturally start to withdraw from others and feel you don't fit in either camp. This can be a fairly painful process, and not just because you might feel lonely or isolated. In addition, you might also feel very humbled as you recognize some of your own patterns of behavior that have held you in judgment and criticism.

When external acceptance is less important, you start to see how you have contributed to the oppression of yourself and even others. Perhaps you used to engage in gossip circles, and now you see those words for the harm they actually caused. It's less important to you to compare jobs, relationships, and parenting achievements than it used to be. These things just don't feed your spirit any longer.

That's not to say you can't find support from friendship and family ties, rather that as you begin the process of self-acceptance, your needs change. You will likely find that you want to surround yourself with others who are also managing their own energy and focusing on their own personal development. The changes within you will be apparent to those around you, and it will feel like *everyone* has an opinion about what **They** think is best. Be sure to define the **They**.

EVEN IF THE PEOPLE AROUND YOU DON'T CHANGE, THE WAY YOU INTERACT WITH THEM WILL.

As a result, your old methods for sustaining relationships may not suffice any longer. Even if the people around you don't change, the way you interact with them will. On top of that you will add new people to your life — those that are comfortable with your new shift in perception and who can be of great support as it unfolds.

Some relationships may fall away, and it is not the end of the world. I've often heard it said that people come into our lives for "a reason, a season, or a lifetime." If you see a relationship ending as a result of your own personal development, you may need to examine it to see if it falls into one of the first two categories. That doesn't mean you shouldn't honor it for what it was. You can cherish those fun times and carry the great memories with you, accepting them as the gift that they were. Perhaps the relationship will transform into something even more fulfilling, or perhaps it will serve as a lesson (the reason) or an important part of a particular stage of life (the season).

PEOPLE COME INTO OUR LIVES FOR "A REASON, A SEASON, OR A LIFETIME."

In my case, this shift in relationships lasted for about three years, as I was transitioning from my previous way of doing things and my corporate identity into my role as a **Recovering Alpha Female**. I was disheartened at times when I would see my old friends going off to the beach together. I longed for the invitation to THE party of the year. I missed the sense of popularity that came along with these types of activities and feeling included.

But, I was also beginning to take root in my new life. I recognized that those activities weren't what I really needed to nurture my spirit. When I did attend the events, I felt like I was wearing a scarlet letter that marked me as "weird" or "unproductive." I was still in the grasp of worrying about what **They** thought. The external me was looking for the "atta girl," or to run down the achiever checklist, but the internal me was thirsting for real connections.

As I chose to nurture my desire for those connections, the social invitations began to fall away. I had less to do and a whole lot more time in which to do it. To be honest, I often felt awkward and unproductive. This phase still ebbs and flows, however, as I learn to honor myself and find the power in the present moment, I find that I am engaging with people who also cherish me and synergize with my evolution. I am able to better recognize those people who are friends for life. Definitely quality versus quantity!

When you devote yourself to being kinder and more compassionate, you find that these kinds of friends don't necessarily have to be sought out. Instead, you are brought together on an energetic level. These are the people with whom you feel a heart connection. You don't have to prove, defend, or justify yourself.

YOU WILL FIND A DECREASE IN THE QUANTITY OF YOUR RELATIONSHIPS BUT A WONDERFUL INCREASE IN THEIR QUALITY.

By my own previous standards, I may have moved into a category of weird, but I was blessed to note that those who came to me were also weird in all the right ways. This was my new **baseline of "normal,"** and it was a much more fulfilling one than I had in my previous gotta-go-gotta-work-gotta-be-the-best lifestyle. You will find that this shift culminates in a decrease in the *quantity* of relationships but in a wonderful increase in their *quality*.

What makes more sense to you: a lot of surface relationships that fill your time and keep you from developing into the person you were meant to be, or a handful of true friends who support your spirit and **Hold Space** for your unfolding? Which of these things should really be considered normal?

Surrounding yourself with **people who are as normal as you** happens both consciously and effortlessly — the connection comes energetically.

BE YOU-NIQUE

UNIQUE. YOU-NIQUE. THEY ARE PRONOUNCED THE SAME, THROUGH A WONDERFUL COINCIDENCE OF OUR CURIOUS ENGLISH LANGUAGE. The **Recovering Alpha Female** is ready to expand her thinking patterns, and one simple way to do so is to readjust how we look at this one word. More so, however, there is inherent power in how we apply it to ourselves.

Being YOU-nique means celebrating your authentic self, appreciating your true nature. This isn't about what **They** see or want you to be, but about what you already are. It's about the fact that you are special, and you don't need external accolades to tell you so. The culture we live in is rife with the idea that we — especially women — should remain small. Heck, even our physical beings are supposed to be as waif-like as possible. It's hard to get a clearer metaphor for how we are expected to also keep our thoughts and inner light from becoming too large.

It was hard for me to allow myself to be **YOU-nique**. Sure, I thought I was special; but that was usually based on other people telling me I was special. I was so good at my job, I had such a talent for decorating, I was doing a great job of raising my children in a Christian way. Really, though, these validations were not about my uniqueness, rather they were about my ability to meet other people's expectations — to fit in!

It wasn't until after my divorce that I really started to internalize my own **YOU-niqueness.** I was experiencing a lot of sadness and anger at this point, and I would allow myself to wallow in it. After all, if I could tell myself that my feelings were based on all these external factors, it would allow me to avoid really delving any deeper into their true cause.

IF I WAS SPECIAL IT WAS BECAUSE OTHER PEOPLE TOLD ME I WAS.

One day, two painful years into the divorce process, I found myself outside with the kids. They were playing on the grass as I swept the garage (always keeping busy, right?). For a fleeting moment, I smiled to myself and thought, "Wow. I'm doing really well right now."

This joyful thought was quickly extinguished by a mind that chastised me for my lack of humility. Feeling that way was arrogant and boastful. At that moment, however, a small crack appeared in the wall between my true self and the world around me. A ray of light poured in, and it shone directly upon a falsehood that had been ingrained in me and so many others.

The realization that followed centered on the contradiction between what we are supposed to want and how we are supposed to get it. We are constantly encouraged to seek the approval of others, to be desirous of and grateful for their praise for our accomplishments. On the other hand, if we recognize and celebrate those same accomplishments in ourselves, it is considered arrogant. How can we shine at our brightest when we're really only allowed to glow as much as someone else is willing to allow or fuel?

This was an eye-opening moment for me. I found myself grieving for our young people, realizing that they are trained from day one to meet others' expectations rather than to see their own inherent worth. Instead of focusing on a life that is fulfilling and spiritually satisfying, they are browbeaten into maintaining the appearance that everything is perfect. And so, they grow up to be **Alpha Adults,** just as I did…and likely, just as you did, too.

ARE YOU PERFORMING FOR THE EXTERNAL WORLD, OR ARE YOU FEEDING YOUR SOUL AND YOUR SPIRIT?

Take a moment to think about the ways that your life is going well. Then, ask yourself whose definition of "going well" you're using. Is it your own, or is it what **They** say you should be doing? Are you performing for the external world, or are you feeding your soul and your spirit?

When I asked myself these questions, I wasn't exactly thrilled by my own answers. I discovered that a whole lot of what I was doing was in an effort to get the thumbs up from society, from family and friends. It was important to me that **They** approve. It was astonishing to realize that I wasn't driven by my own desires, but by those of others. Acceptance and approval was more important to me than finding my own self worth. Don't get me wrong, I was certainly successful when measured against the high bar of achievements, but the problem was that I completely ignored my **YOU-nique** spirit in order to reach that level.

Instead of nourishing myself, I was constantly doing things from a place of "should." I like to say that I was "shoulding" all over myself. (It's funnier if you say it out loud.) Sure, some of what I was doing was important, but because I was always coming from the "should" perspective, it just became rote behavior for me. There was no thinking involved. I was not expressing myself at all. I was simply going through the motions of life.

I had to be really patient with myself in order to get past this. Life went ahead and threw in a few of those **humbling blocks** to help me get the message. For example, even though I thought I was doing something for myself and trying to make the world a better place by teaching yoga, reality hit me like a sledge hammer when I injured myself. As I struggled with my recovery and the depression that it brought, I realized that even this aspect of my life had been about the external reward. I had wanted so much to be the perfect example that I pushed myself harder than I knew I should. The universe saw this and sent me a big, fat "Nuh-uh!" in the form of a herniated disc.

After a lot of rewiring and patience, I have gotten to a point where I now realize that I absolutely must live in the moment. I consciously choose my thoughts and actions. If I am doing something because I "should" or because it's what **They** say is right, I notice and make course corrections when appropriate. Just as it is helpful to redefine the word "unique," it is also a good idea to take a look at our own definition of the word "right" as a part of this process of awakening.

Embracing my **YOU-niqueness** led to some uncomfortable moments. When I first tried to express myself honestly, my words would often come out bold or harsh. I was trying to speak in a totally new way, almost as if I was communicating in a foreign language, and the results tended to be very reactive. I had been conditioned to express myself as every good little girl was expected to — doing what I was told and not speaking out of turn. When I realized that it was OK, even preferable, to allow myself to be angry or to say what I felt initially, I didn't quite have the tools to do it in the most gracious manner.

My early attempts to express myself authentically were rough around the edges, to say the least. I would just let my feelings out in whatever form they happened to take. I would compare it to a baby learning to walk. My steps (or words) were shaky and probably a bit unstable, but I had determination to see myself through the awkward, wobbly parts, knowing that when I got to the other side, my world would be much more accessible and authentic and I would be that much more independent.

I definitely encourage those interested in living more authentically to accept the struggle that comes with this part of the experience. I realize that being wobbly and

EXPRESSING OURSELVES IS THE ONLY WAY WE HAVE TO DISPLAY OUR FEELINGS TO OTHERS.

vulnerable is not something that appeals to most Alpha Female types, but it is part of the process. By the time I was learning how to speak more authentically, it was just me and my three children in the home; and those poor kids sometimes found themselves on the receiving end of a blow torch of whatever emotion I was trying to get out.

That, in and of itself, offered a whole new **humbling block**. When I would speak unkind words to my children, I had to override my self-delusions of perfection in order to apologize to them. I would explain to them that I was trying really hard to break old patterns and that I was fumbling around while learning how. Their acceptance of my apologies made it easier for me to accept them from myself, and we would often end up laughing while we all practiced speaking our own truths. We learned together how to let our emotions out through our words, rather than stuffing them all back down into the darkness within.

Expressing ourselves — verbally, through art, with our actions, etc. — is the only way we have to display our feelings to others. To embrace this is to embrace your own **YOU-niqueness**. It is a method for giving yourself the grace required to explore your own gifts, to claim them as your own, and to walk away when you know it's the right choice for you. Maybe things will come out a little ugly at the beginning, but it is a process; and by staying with it, you will find that you are learning to express the good things in an authentic way.

In doing these things, you will also learn how to give yourself pause before reacting to stimuli. After you've screwed up a few (or a lot of) times, you begin to learn how to **reflect rather than react.** To choose your responses instead of just letting them fall out of your mouth. It gives you the ability to inspire grace and love for yourself that ripples out to others through the mere happenstance of being near you. When this happens, you know that you are walking the walk that is yours, not just following in someone else's footsteps because you "should." You are allowing yourself to be **YOU-nique**.

FENG SHUI
YOUR DAY

YOU MAY HAVE HEARD OF FENG SHUI AND BE REALLY ON BOARD WITH THE IDEA OF HOW YOU CAN DIRECT ENERGY TO FLOW THE MOST EFFECTIVELY THROUGH YOUR HOME. Or, you might just think it looks really nice to organize and display things a certain way. Or, maybe you don't have a clue what **Feng Shui** is all about. None of those options really matter when it comes to this **ah-ha**, because it's more about arranging your life than your furniture.

One of the biggest hurdles that a **Recovering Alpha Female** experiences is that of time. Just about everyone laments that there's not enough time in a day to do all the things they want, but the Alpha Female takes this challenge head on, thumbs her nose at it, and somehow gets it all done anyway. Do you hear what I'm saying? The Alpha Female takes it upon herself to do things that are just a shade short of impossible. And she does them well.

How exhausting! How stressful! How really, really unnecessary!

When you go into Alpha Female Recovery, it's time to admit that you can't — or shouldn't — do it all. I was a single mother who was performing Herculean feats when it came to time management. Everyone was benefitting from the fact that I could juggle competing deadlines, that I would rather do something myself than to take the time to teach someone else how to do it right, that I would stay up late at night to sweat the details. Everyone, that is, but me.

Of course, I didn't realize it at the time. I was having my ego stroked and patting myself on the back for my ability to do it all.

Once I determined that I needed to make some changes, letting go of this ability was an unexpected challenge. What would I do if every moment of every day wasn't crammed full of distractions and activity? How was I going to survive moving at a slower pace?

For me, it came down to accepting **progress over perfection.** This is a bitter pill to swallow at first — if you *can* do it all (yeah, right), then why *wouldn't* you do it all? I can think of a few reasons:

- Because you miss out on precious moments with those who are the most important to you.
- Because you stifle the whispers of your heart.
- Because you make yourself physically ill.
- Because you make yourself mentally ill.

- Because you become jaded and resentful.
- BECAUSE PURSUIT OF PERFECTION SETS YOU UP FOR FAILURE.

These are just a few of the reasons to stop the frantic need to go full speed ahead at all times. The last item on that list bears repeating, however: Perfection sets you up for failure. No matter what you do, it will never be absolutely perfect. There will always be that one slightly crooked line in your drawing, the missed stitch in the hem of your kid's Halloween costume, a raise at work that you're sure you deserve. Because there is no such thing as perfection, aiming for it means that

IF YOU ARE TRYING FOR PERFECTION, YOU WILL NEVER REACH YOUR GOAL.

you will miss hitting it 100% of the time. Imagine that. The person who is most likely to create something wonderful (the Alpha Female) is setting herself up for failure 100% of the time. No wonder we don't see our own worth; we think we're failures at every single thing we do.

And so, I choose the mantra, "Progress, not perfection." If you are trying for perfection, you will never reach your goal. If you are trying for progress, you will succeed.

Feng Shui Your Day is about how to make this progress in a meaningful way. It's about allowing — possibly even ordering — yourself to do one small thing each day that brings you personal satisfaction and a sense of your own accomplishment. It's not about the external rewards and validation, it's about nurturing your own spirit.

Maybe you have a junk drawer that needs to be cleaned out. Maybe you've long been planning to hang new curtains in the bedroom. Maybe you just want to read a book for the sheer enjoyment of it, rather than because it will look impressive while you're sitting at the coffee shop or because Oprah recommended it. The key to this is to do something that will make YOU happy. Will it make you feel good to open that junk drawer the next time and be able to easily find what you're looking for instead of rifling through a bunch of pocket change, ink pens, rubber bands, orphaned screws, unwrapped candies, etc, etc? No one else is going to see the inside of that drawer, so if you choose to clean it, do it for your own happiness.

As I was starting my journey as a **Recovering Alpha Female**, I had to take some baby steps. One of those was to touch up all the black marks on the wall going up the stairwell and into the mud room. Dirty fingerprints and random stains abounded, and I decided that I was going to fix it, just for me. Here's the catch, I didn't do a perfect job of it. Because there is no such thing as perfection, right? The paint color was a smidge off. Still, it looked better than the black marks had, and that made me feel good. I lived with it for a while, and the good feelings it produced eventually led me to launch into the process of painting the inside of my house in my favorite colors.

Painting is a pretty cheap way to give your home a facelift, and if you get the wrong color — so what? **It's just paint!** And you know what? It felt so good.

I'm not suggesting that you need to run out and buy gallons of paint, rather I'm trying to make the point that there are so many little tasks we put off for whatever reason. It might be that you don't have time in your Alpha Female schedule of meeting everyone else's needs to actually attend to your own. It's also possible that you're scared — of making the wrong choice, of not doing a perfect job, of discovering you just really aren't any good at painting — or whatever it is you've chosen to do.

As a **Recovering Alpha Female**, however, you are able to see past those self-imposed barriers. You may still not have a lot of extra time in your day, but — again, you're looking for progress, not perfection. So what if it takes you three days to get that junk drawer into shape? So what if you won't do a perfect job? So what if you find out you're not quite as crafty as you'd hoped? So what? On the other hand, what if you do a good enough job that you smile every time you walk past your new eggplant-colored walls? What if you realize that you

kind of love using your hot glue gun or — dare I say it?
— organizing your cupboards and drawers?

Feng Shui Your Day isn't about money, either. If you
can't afford to paint the walls or buy art supplies or
whatever, that's OK. When I started this process, I
couldn't afford much. I made myself extremely happy
by purchasing a couple of colorful pens and Sharpies. I
loved them so much and called them my **"highlighters
and happy pens,"** taking them everywhere with
me. An even less expensive option is to give yourself
permission to take a relaxing bath. If you've got a
candle, light it and just enjoy the water and allow
yourself to breathe.

One of the most fun things I ever did was to have a
trusted friend come over and help me clean my closet.
She was honest and ruthless, and when we were done,
I had a box full of things I didn't need that could be
removed from my life. I wasn't necessarily prepared
to fully let those unworn blouses and status-symbol
handbags go, so I put them in the garage. There was
no pressure to let it go. I was so energized by the
calm, clean space in my closet, that I found myself
purging and uncluttering other areas of my life, too. It
was so satisfying!

Consider making yourself a list of small things you
could do that would make you happy. Once a day, pick
one of those things and do it. You will be amazed at

how your current lack of time begins to expand, making room for these "just for me" opportunities. You will never find perfection, but if you **Feng Shui** Your Day, you will see progress!

IF YOU HAVE TO FIGHT TO FIT, IT'S THE WRONG FIT

IT SEEMS LIKE HUMAN NATURE WANTS US SO DESPERATELY TO FIT IN WITH THE CROWD. We are always looking for affirmation that others actually want to be around us, to feel a sense of belonging and community. So many times, though, we strive for this for all the wrong reasons. Our desire to fit into the physical world, the family circles and friend groups, all too often is about feeling worthy. We want proof that we are respected by others and that we have value. In fact, we want it so badly that even if it feels wrong to us, we pursue it anyway. We struggle and fight for relationships that ultimately cause us to ignore the feelings in our heart.

Family connections are somewhat revered in our culture, but they are also some of the hardest to sustain. I say this with incredible amounts of love because I happen to have a truly amazing family. Still, my personal quest for unconditional self-acceptance has sometimes strained familial relationships. As I have branched off and realized that I have to walk in my own truth, my circumstances have changed, and that has been hard for some of the family to accept.

HAVE YOU EVER WORN A PAIR OF SHOES SIMPLY BECAUSE THEY WERE GORGEOUS, EVEN THOUGH THEY DIDN'T FIT RIGHT?

There is no doubt that my family loves and supports me, but that doesn't mean that they approve of or understand all of my choices. For example, I took a break from the religion of my childhood. This was hard for them to understand and at times required me to remove myself from family situations.

One of the best and worst things about family is that they hold you to your old story. This is a blessing because you have these people with whom you share so many common experiences. Your histories are intertwined, and they are full of love for who you've been. On the other hand, it can be confusing and frustrating to them to see you change. If they remember the insecure little girl who always wanted to be the center of attention, it can be very difficult for them to reconcile that image with the new, confident woman who speaks her own truth and doesn't continually seek their approval.

Your growth can cause you to sprout a new branch on the family tree. Sure, you still all have the same roots, but you've begun to grow in a new direction, reaching for the light. It can be hard for them to accept this evolution, and you may find that you are no longer fitting in with your family and their established patterns. In fact, this may become true in regards to your friends, your religious beliefs, your political leanings, your community and society in general.

This can be painful and you may feel like you are being rejected. In my case, I found that as my inner strength grew, I realized that I wanted to rekindle, foster, and nurture an old relationship. The other person didn't understand the changes in me and chose to keep his cards very close to his chest. When I reached out, he refused to engage with me. I felt crushed by this and would often cry myself to sleep, lost in memories of the good times we used to share. No matter how hard I tried, I could not force the relationship to fit.

YOUR GROWTH CAN CAUSE YOU TO GROW IN NEW DIRECTIONS.

The awkwardness of a poor fit can be pretty clear, but we sometimes try to play through the pain anyway. Have you ever worn a pair of shoes simply because they were gorgeous, even though they didn't fit right? By the end of the evening, you're limping and might even have to take them off, and you spend the next several days tending to the blisters and sore skin. Staying in a relationship that doesn't fit is similar. It may look great and make you feel good for a short time, but eventually you're going to suffer for it.

A GOOD EXAMPLE OF THIS COMES IN THE WAKE OF A DIVORCE. In trying to fill an

emptiness, many people will jump right into a new relationship, often with someone who has the same frustrations as the one they've left. They're still trying to make the old relationship fit, even though it clearly won't. Sure, there's a sexiness to something new, but in the end, it's just a repeat of trying to fight to make it fit.

As your personal awareness grows, you will start to carry yourself a bit differently. You will walk the planet with a little more intention. You will begin to feel more comfortable and confident in your own skin. This is a great time to choose personal development over an attempt to try and force a fit that is never going to happen. As old relationships fall away, it is a perfect opportunity to relearn (or unlearn) your beliefs regarding what makes a relationship succeed or fail. Instead, it's time to examine what your real needs are and what traits will help you meet them.

The next step is to embody these traits yourself. After all, if they're something you think is important in others, then they're probably important in you, too. Also, like attracts like. There's no better way to have the kinds of friends you want than to be the kind of friend you want. Finally, there's no one in the world you spend more time with than yourself. Why wouldn't you want to hang out with someone who exhibits all the best qualities and is a better fit for you? Learn to be your own best friend.

When this starts to feel lonely, I turn to my audiobooks. Thank you, Carolyn Myss, Wayne Dyer, Don Miguel, and Pema Chodron for being my constant companions and support when I felt isolated — like I was a freak and didn't belong. These authors didn't even know they supported me, that they held space for me. In fact, they still often do.

FORGET
"THE FAIRYTALE"

THIS AH-HA IS SHORT AND SWEET, BUT IT'S ALSO VERY POWERFUL.

From the time we are tiny little humans, we are inundated with the idea that we should strive for The Fairytale life. Yes, The Fairytale is beautiful, and we can all achieve aspects of it. But, the chances of being born a princess or being discovered by a talent scout or inventing the next big thing and becoming a millionaire are actually pretty small.

That doesn't mean that it's not OK to dream about The Fairytale. What is far more effective, though, is to participate in it. If there are things you want in life, put them on your radar and move toward them. The most realistic way to do this is to have a vision of what you want without being hopelessly attached to the idea that you will get it. Remember, this is about what you *truly* want, not about what **They** say you *should* want. So much of The Fairytale we try to achieve isn't even our own! If you play an active role in creating your own fairytale, your subconscious mind will help to bring it to life. It will notice the small things and encourage you to utilize them to bring your dreams to reality.

One of the ways to do this is to create vision boards. You might include things like your financial goals, what you want in a relationship, and *how* you want to be, rather than just *what* you want to be. What types of adventure do you seek? Put those on there, as well. Your vision boards should serve as tools to spark the subconscious to be drawn to the right things, to share your hopes and dreams with the universe while you are involved in the work of the present. When you stay in the moment, you are so much more likely to recognize the opportunities that surround you every day. Multi-tasking is no longer on the top of the achievement list.

A cool part of this is that you may find that things you previously saw as blocking your dreams can actually play a role in manifesting them. When you are open to the positive, you're more likely to see it. Maybe you've been in a relationship that you felt was boring, but when you look at it from a new perspective, you realize that this person is offering you quite a lot. Instead of always looking for The Fairytale, don't be afraid to find it in your own life.

If a marriage or other long-term relationship ends, as women we think the next step is to jump right into a new relationship, but I would encourage my fellow **RAF**'s to take a little time to get to know themselves first. Get to know your quirks (Colors as I call them). Get to know your passions. Get comfortable being alone and not "doing." After my divorce, I began seeking a husband right away, thinking that was what I was supposed to do and it was what I needed to help me raise the kids. Basically, I was afraid to be alone.

YOU SHOULD NOT DETERMINE YOUR OWN VALUE BASED ON WHETHER OR NOT YOUR "FAIRYTALE" COMES TRUE.

My first relationship after the divorce was with a great guy. He was cute, good with kids, and younger! We had a lot of fun together. Things were starting to line up on paper. I asked him, "So, how are you going to take care of us?" and was dismayed when he replied, "I'm not. I'm just having fun." My question freaked him out, and his response freaked me out! It was at that moment that I recognized that I needed to take care of myself. This is when I began to create my own fairytale.

Forget The Fairytale doesn't mean that you can't believe in or look forward to something bigger and more suitable. What it does mean is that you need to lead your life in a way that makes the fairytale possible. Forget The Fairytale also means that you should not determine your own value based on whether or not it comes true.

It very well may not feel like your life has been a fairytale up to this point, but we shouldn't overlook the fact that each experience we've had has been one from which we can draw inspiration and a better understanding of both ourselves and the world around us. How wonderful would it be to look back at certain "bubbles" of time that didn't necessarily turn out the way we hoped, and instead of feeling remorse or disappointment, feeling happiness for the brilliance that they contained — for the gifts they provided in the form of insight? In my case, who would have thought that such a scary disease and difficult divorce would launch this personal journey?

There's a quote from Dr. Seuss that pertains as much to adults as it does to children: "Don't cry because it's over. Smile because it happened." Of course, there are deep emotions attached to past experiences, and not all of them make us feel good. But, each and every thing we've gone through is a potential building block toward our own rewritten and redefined fairytale. Participate and start dreaming your own.

CHUCK THE CHECKLIST

AS I SAT IN THE CHAIR, RECEIVING AN IV TREATMENT FOR MS, MY EMOTIONS BATTLED ONE ANOTHER, WITH THEIR SWORDS AND DAGGERS DRAWN, SLASHING AND STABBING. It felt impossible for me to get out of my own way at moments like that. On the one hand, I am an Alpha Female. I had to be strong, have it all together, and avoid showing any sign of weakness. When I was done with the infusion, I would impress everyone with my ability to remain mobile, to go home and keep a so-called normal life balanced and running at full speed.

On the outside, I would appear to be polite and understanding, while my blood was boiling with frustration. The medical staff would have to try one vein after another after another before finally being able to insert the needle effectively. No one would know how exposed and vulnerable I truly felt, because I was not about to show this 'weak' side. I would silently do the math. *I'm 45 now. How many more years of this treatment will I be able to take? And how bad is the alternative going to be?*

On the outside, I was strong. I was the model patient, the example of not letting your disease get the best of you. On the inside, I was so utterly fatigued, afraid of immobility, and terribly alone. Playing the victim card was easy — "Look at this terrible disease that has happened to me... Look how well I am holding up..." What I couldn't say out loud was, "Why isn't anyone visiting me or bringing me dinner?" Really, I wanted to just cry and often did so, but quietly so others wouldn't know. I wanted to just feel sorry for myself and be a little pitiful sometimes. But, that did not fit into the persona of that totally together, Type-A woman I projected.

On the inside, I had a checklist of what I should do and what other people should do.

I should:

- Not complain
- Be an example
- Remember that others have it worse than I
- Not let treatment slow me down
- Not ask for help

Others should:

- Acknowledge me for not complaining
- Recognize that I am an example
- Hit the vein in one poke

- **Hold Space** for me to feel sad
- Read my mind about coming to visit me or needing help, help with the kids or bring dinner by.

You can probably see how these two lists would clash and create separation. The most important aspect for the **Recovering Alpha Female** to realize, of course, is how those last items conflicted in such a way as to make sure my expectations would never be met.

How could those around me provide the comfort and reassurances that I craved when I made it so clear that I didn't need them? **They** were doing exactly what I wanted, if **They** went by my outward appearances. How's that for a Catch-22? I wouldn't ask for help, and then I would cry over not getting it. If I did express a desire for some sort of assistance, it would often be accompanied by feelings of resentment that others hadn't thought of it on their own. Just like the thing about there being no such thing as perfection, I was setting myself (and others) up to fail most of the time.

I think a lot of us are carrying around checklists with items that contradict one another.

For example:

- Earn tons of money or have more free time
- Be invited to lots of parties or have good quality time with kids
- Stay fit and work out hard or find more quiet, relaxing time.

Sure, you can have more free time after you earn the money, but you're going to have to put in the hours now to make it happen. It's borderline impossible to make both of these things happen at the same time, and anyone who tells you differently is probably trying to get you to sign up for their pyramid scheme.

I'm not saying that it isn't helpful to have a to-do list, because that would be patently untrue. It would also contradict what I said in **Feng Shui** Your Day. What I do encourage **Recovering Alpha Females** to do is to take a look at the mental checklists we constantly compare ourselves against and determine if they are really necessary. Is having a fancy car what you really want, or is it what **They** say you should want? Are you taking homemade blueberry muffins to the school bake sale because you love to cook or because you feel like you have to check it off the list in order to be a "good mom?"

Chuck the checklist that someone else has written and be the creator of your own story. I put myself through considerable extra agony during those treatments simply because I was ticking off items on the Inspiring Person with a Chronic Disease checklist that we've all mentally compiled from years of applauding (rightfully so) those who have shown amazing strength in their own medical battles. I wanted to be perceived as that person, even though my heart was quietly whispering to me that I should be writing my own story instead of trying to live up to someone else's.

I sometimes say that I was on a "Heroine Trip." My pride was surely in the way of my own healing because I wanted everyone to think I was a heroine instead of allowing myself to ask for what I actually needed. It took me a very long time to accept the feelings of pain, sadness, and uncertainty I felt; and it took far longer for me to open up about them and my fear for the future to anyone else. In order to do so, I had to chuck the checklist of expectations and settle into authenticity.

My situation was about my MS, raising children according to society's standards, and finding Mr. Right a second time around. Yours is probably about something completely different. But, if you are hoping to become a **Recovering Alpha Female**, you're going to need to examine the checklists that may be governing your life. **Who wrote the list? Did you, or did They?** Because, nine times out of ten, what **They** want doesn't give a single consideration to what is best or right for you.

HOLD SPACE

YOU MAY HAVE NOTICED THROUGHOUT THIS BOOK THAT I KEEP REFERRING TO THE IDEA OF "HOLDING SPACE." This is a concept that sometimes takes some grappling in order to understand, but it a huge component in the journey to becoming a **Recovering Alpha Female**.

Another common theme in these pages is me sharing my personal stories of how and why I implemented the different **ah-ha's** The purpose of this is never to tell you "this is how you should do it;" rather it's to provide context and examples of how it can be done. Your walk is yours, and I am just here to offer some perspectives and permissions, and to **Hold Space**.

Underlying each of these stories are a few common threads. These are the things that I have come to realize were sabotaging my ability to truly let my light shine:

- Feeling that I was NEVER ENOUGH.
- Continually striving for perfection.
- Believing that I didn't belong or fit in.
- Feeling that I was unworthy of unconditional love and acceptance.

Each of these threads has brought into my life a ridiculous amount of self-bullying. The voice in my head would shout over the whispers of my heart to tell me that there was no way that my soul could, or should, ever shine. Why, that would be arrogant.

Thus far, my journey has taken about eight years, with the last four really bringing into focus the fact that I am on a quest for personal discovery. The **humbling blocks** that were put in my path had to create their own pattern for me to be able to recognize how much I was actually struggling.

The good news for you is that as I've moved forward on my own path, I have collected these stories and insights. With nothing but love and encouragement, I am now offering them up to you. Rather than fumbling in the dark as I did for so long, I give you my hard-knocks realizations as a way to find the starting line and to support you as you take things at your own pace. You, my friend, do not necessarily have to reinvent the wheel.

HOLDING SPACE MEANS HONORING YOUR TRANSFORMATIVE PROCESS. It allows you to **reflect instead of react.** Most who take this road are those who have come to realize they simply can't find peace through their current patterns and by blindly following what **They** say is the right course through a modern life. **Hold Space** for yourself. **Be gentle and**

kind to Her because this transformation takes time and practice.

In order to start holding space for yourself, envision a large, open, and beautifully decorated box in your heart. Now, as you unpack your heart, mind, and spirit, allow yourself to place whatever you find into this box. Some of what you find will be pleasant, life-affirming things, such as deeper connections and creative expression. Others may be ugly, like shame and regret. This box, though, is safe. There is no one who can peek into that space to see what is there and judge or criticize you.

When your anger comes out sideways as you're finding your voice, you can put your harshly-spoken words into the box and just let them be without needing to beat yourself up over them. If you are disappointed by a lost love, you can put that into the box, too. You cannot change the past, and holding space for it allows you to honor it in a healthy way.

TOO OFTEN THE RAF SHIFTS INTO PROBLEM-SOLVING MODE, WHEN SHE INSTEAD NEEDS TO JUST HOLD SPACE.

Holding space is not an easy thing for the **Recovering Alpha Female**. As an Alpha, we often become uncomfortable and awkward with silence. If there's a lull in the conversation, for example, we will often rush in. After all, the Alpha Female has an incredibly active mind, and one of the ways that manifests is through conversation. It keeps us busy and focused on the external. So many times in a conversation, the Alpha shifts into problem-solving mode, trying to fix things when perhaps the other person really just needs us to **Hold Space** for them while they share their feelings and insights.

IT'S NO COINCIDENCE THAT "SILENT" AND "LISTEN" ARE SPELLED WITH THE SAME

LETTERS. By allowing ourselves to feel the discomfort of a lull in conversation rather than hurrying to fill the silence with advice, we can create a far more authentic connection in which everyone feels fully heard. And, of course, this is also about being silent and listening to yourself so that you can hear your own inner voice and respond with compassion and acceptance rather than trying to fix everything in the moment. Oh, yes! We Alphas are fixers and problem solvers.

As a part of your own experience, I want to extend an offer to **Hold Space** for you, too. I am attempting to give you not only some possible steps to take, but also the permission you may feel you need to embark. I am telling you that it is OK to turn your attention to uncovering your authentic self. It's OK to be nervous and frightened about what you'll find. It's OK to bring the Alpha Female into balance and start supporting Her — the woman in the mirror. And if you happen to find something that you just can't or don't want to put in your box, give it time. It will come when the time is right.

Throughout the course of my life, I have been many things. Some of these are lovely titles, such as "wife," "mother," "businesswoman," "award winner." Others are not so nice, like "reactive," "control freak," "manipulative." After holding space for all of these titles at one time or another, I can take them all on, knowing that each aspect of myself has brought me to where I am today. And in order to nurture those positive qualities and minimize the negative ones, I make it a daily practice to trust and stay plugged in to the call of my soul and to accept that within it resides infinite wisdom and guidance.

If you will accept it, I am offering my support. I will **Hold Space** for you. I will accept you and encourage you as you make your way through this process of unfolding. Above all, I will join you as you learn to embrace your colorful quirks and occasionally have a laugh at your own expense.

LOOK UP TO YOUR YOUNGERS

OBVIOUSLY, I FEEL LIKE EACH AH-HA IS IMPORTANT, BUT IF I HAD TO CHOOSE JUST ONE FOR YOUNGER WOMEN TO TAKE SERIOUSLY, THIS WOULD BE IT. As an Alpha Female, I had plenty of opportunities for education. I went to college. I attended workshops and seminars. I had on-the-job training. I am self-educated, formally educated, and pretty much everything in between.

All of this is to say that I know a little something about learning. I also know something about teachers. Without a doubt, I can tell you that there has been no better, more challenging, or more profound teacher in my life than my three children. Not only have they taught me patience, compassion, and how to make baby purees in the food processor, but they have also taught me *how* to learn.

Very young children don't learn by reading lessons in books or scratching out arithmetic problems with a pencil and paper. That's not how learning to walk, talk, and hold a spoon happen. I would argue that even as they get older, the most important lessons still have little to do with memorizing the periodic table or diagramming sentences. Realistically, children learn by watching, by observing. They learn by observing us.

If you look back on your own Alpha Female tendencies, you may find that they started through observation and emulation of the adults in your life. Maybe they were always on the go or you were constantly vying with siblings for your parents' attention. Maybe it was precisely the opposite: you saw your parents struggling to make ends meet and promised yourself not to live that way. The children around you are currently watching you in the same way. They are internalizing how you interact with loved ones, how you treat others on the phone, and how you hide from the religious callers

CHILDREN ARE INNATELY INTUITIVE AND SO CONNECTED TO THEIR AUTHENTIC SELVES

when you really are at home. They are learning from you while you are learning from them.

But looking up to someone isn't the same as learning from them. It has more to do with respecting them, seeing their wisdom, and honoring it. It is ingrained in us from early on that we should respect our elders. After all, they have a whole lifetime of knowledge that we don't yet have. They have done and learned things that we can respect, as well as learn from. Just the mere fact of their existence on this planet means that we should at the very least respect them as another sentient being.

I've known this pretty much my whole life, and you probably have, too. It was actually my son who turned this idea on its head and gave me a new perspective. One evening as we were snuggling after he'd spent a fun-filled day with his grandparents, he shared with me that he'd gotten into a little bit of trouble with them for not following directions immediately. I started in with the standard lecture about how children should look up to their elders. How you should listen no matter what because they're adults and we need to respect them.

My eight-year-old boy sat straight up in bed, fit to be tied. "Mom!" he exclaimed. "People should just look up to their **youngers**!" I laughed for a moment but then realized what a profound idea that was. Children are innately intuitive and so connected to their authentic selves, and yet we work like mad to raise them the way we were raised. I'm not saying this is at all bad, but I do think there's something to be said for breaking old patterns and conditioning. I want my children to feel empowered to be themselves and love themselves, without basing it on performance or achievement.

I would suggest that all of the aspects of respecting someone should apply to the little ones in our lives, too. Even though they may not have been around as long as the rest of us, they still literally have a *lifetime* of experiences. So what if their lifetime is only five or twelve or nineteen years? To them, it is the entirety of known existence.

While our elders have had the opportunity to learn many things throughout their longer lifetimes, children have something completely different to offer because they have not yet *unlearned* many things. As we grow up and are conditioned by family systems, indoctrinated into religious and political beliefs, and molded to fit societal norms, we necessarily leave behind childish notions. Looking up to your **youngers** means to recognize and celebrate those things.

Take for example when a child tries a new food that she doesn't like. An infant will spit it out. A toddler will refuse to eat it. A young child will act as if the world is going to end if it were to pass her lips. A teenager will start to be more subtle, not wanting to offend the chef and may hide the offensive food in her napkin. By the time we're adults, we learn to smile politely and eat the item anyway.

Why is this, exactly? You still don't like the food; but you've determined that it is more important to spare the other person's feelings than to simply say, "No, thank you." Children are generally so much more honest when it comes to their own desires. They are not yet burdened with guilt over wanting something, nor do they feel arrogant for taking pride in their accomplishments.

The Alpha Female has internalized the lessons taught throughout childhood and taken them to the extreme. While there is value in not insulting another person's cooking or choosing not to be a braggart about every little accomplishment, we can still learn from our **youngers** what it means to be in touch with our authentic selves.

WHEN YOU SHIFT AND EXPAND YOUR THINKING, YOU CAN PARENT WITH INTENT AND TRUST.

As a parent, I have had to examine the choices I make in raising my children. I don't wish for them to grow up with the same relentless Alpha tendencies I've worked so hard to balance. Unfortunately, as I've gone through this transition, it hasn't always been pretty for them. My children have been the innocent bystanders to some of my most crazed, fear-ridden moments, before and during my journey.

When they were little, they loved me so fiercely that they were devastated when I was angry with them. They were truly repentant over the fact that they had tracked mud on the floor or spilled milk on the table, because it upset me so much. They deeply felt the moments when I would lose it. And I would eventually feel horrible about it. Was it really that big of a deal for me to grab a towel and clean up the spilled milk? Probably not. But in the heat of the moment, I lashed out at that lack of control. It was something that needed to come to a screeching halt.

Please, let me take a pause here to point out very clearly that I am not a perfect parent. You are not a perfect parent. Those of us who are raising children with intention spend an excruciating amount of time and energy second-guessing our choices. Throwing in a healthy dose of respect for them as autonomous human beings makes things even harder!

Why was I freaking out over the muddy boots and toppled milk in the bedroom? Because these things launched me into the future — the smell of spilled milk, cleaning up the mess, and the work ahead... It also made me mad. The anger gave rise to fear that I wasn't good enough or keeping up with the Joneses, and that led to me biting their heads off. It cut off that little heart whisper that tried to pipe up and tell me to be gentle and come from love. To think of the joy they were having...

When I began to listen to those murmurs and whispers with an open mind, when I started to move toward this life of self-acceptance and trusting my inner knowing, I found that my relationship with my children changed. I continued to do the best I knew how for them, but I also began to do better for myself. Once I put myself back on my priority list, life got better for them. I was much better able to give them the respect they deserved.

What goes unnoticed, however, is that you are a person with your own intrinsic value, and you deserve to be fulfilled. Just as our elders earn respect by the mere fact of their existence, so do we. And — here's where it gets better — when you become more fulfilled, when you learn to be more yourself, your children actually do benefit. When you know who you are and why you believe the way you do, it suddenly becomes a lot easier to make decisions based on reason and personal ethics instead of out of fear or by relying on the default setting of what **They** say you should do.

When you shift and expand your thinking, you can parent with intent and trust. Instead of constantly trying to instill in them how to perform, to keep up, to be better than someone else, you can actually teach them to be true to themselves without apology. And, because you've been learning the same, you are an excellent role model for how it's done.

A big part of this comes back around to looking up to your **youngers**. While I've focused on parenting, this type of systematic change in perception can apply to so many facets of life. Look to the younger folks to learn how to explore and accept your inner knowing. Recognize the joy that is inherent in those who have not yet been taught to knock themselves off of their own priority lists.

The exciting part of this is that you don't even have to apply your understanding blindly. You can integrate aspects of child-like self-acceptance, while tempering it with an adult understanding of how to interact in society. And, you can be realistic. While a child might melt down at being denied something he or she wants, you may be in a better position to accept that reality with grace.

Or, maybe you won't. Maybe you'll spend all day lovingly making a special dinner for your kids, only to have them turn up their noses and cry, "Yuck!" Instead of the kudos and thanks you were expecting or hoping for, you've gotten precisely the opposite. Your choices are to respond in a loving manner, perhaps taking a few moments to reflect and choose your words before launching into your constructive conversation about the perils of starving children in Africa. Or, you can flip your lid, tell the kids to order a damn pizza then, and lock yourself in the bathroom with a bottle of wine.

And you know what? Both of these are OK. If you do the latter, you may want to eventually come back and explain yourself and offer an apology. Your children will see that you are not perfect, and by extension, that means they don't have to be perfect either. But, they also see that you are willing to own your mistakes and ask for forgiveness. Both of these are great lessons, not just for them, but to keep you humble and moving in the right direction, too.

When I started trying to live this way — to reflect rather than react, whether with my children, friends, coworkers, etc. — I may have been successful one time out of ten. This was a big change. I had to go from being the one with all the answers to a person who was willing to examine a situation, take in additional information, integrate it alongside my own beliefs, and then respond. I would compare it to developing a puny little muscle. At first I could lift a feather, and I had to accept that was all I could do. But, as I stretched and exercised it, I got better and better at reflecting rather than reacting.

The results were stunning, too, by the way. While my kids will certainly still fight from time to time, I don't immediately take it as a personal affront. My Alpha Female self isn't triggered by the inability to control them, and the result has been more peace in our home. When I realized the importance of looking up to my **youngers**, I made myself someone more worthy of looking up to, as well.

EPILOGUE
MOVING INTO GRACE

THE ULTIMATE OUTCOME OF ALL OF THIS IS FOR EACH OF US TO MOVE INTO OUR OWN PLACE OF GRACE. It is, of course, important to give grace to others, but the **Recovering Alpha Female** recognizes that she needs to give it to herself, too. A Place of Grace is one where you find yourself settling into your own essence. You are better able to respond to situations with reflection rather than knee-jerk reactions. Instead of reacting harshly to a disappointment or perceived failure, you can pause and retreat to this place while you get your bearings and choose the way you want to respond. A Place of Grace is one in which you can walk a little more softly, where you give yourself permission to let go and simply be still for awhile.

Sometimes, your Place of Grace allows you "nothing time." Nothing time is when you let everything go and just take solace in yourself for a bit. It's an amazing way to recharge, not to mention the fact that it's also when you are most likely to hear the whispers of your heart. Throughout the course of a normal day, we are amped up and ramped up and running from one thing to the next. In the Place of Grace, though, it is possible to become an observer instead of a participant. We can suspend judgment and simply look at the situation with curiosity and wonder.

This ability to remove ourselves from the action also means that our Place of Grace allows us to accept others as they are. We can let them have their own story, rather than trying to interject ourselves or our expectations into the situation. We can simply provide them with unconditional love on their journeys as they grow and evolve in their own ways. It allows you to **Hold Space** for that person, too.

For example, let's say it's a typical hectic day in the life of a family. Kids are running late to school, homework's not done, there's music practice and sports to fit into the schedule this afternoon. It's overwhelming, to say the least. Add to that your own impatience or disappointment that your kids aren't doing as they "should," and it gets pretty easy to explode and even let the Alpha Female take over to get stuff done the way you want it.

Knowing that you have that Place of Grace, though, can provide a way for you to back away from the situation emotionally. You can **Hold Space** for your children and their current inability to manage their time wisely. Sure, it's your job to help them learn those skills, but what's done for today is done for today. Holding space for those aspects of your kids' personalities where they might struggle allows you to accept them as they are while offering support as they unfold in their own ways. They become better equipped to make their own choices, develop a sense of responsibility, and trust their knowing with your loving guidance rather than scorn and disappointment.

As we become more empowered in our own development, we find it more and more comfortable to take a step back and allow others to become empowered, too. As you learn to trust your inner wisdom and knowing, you recognize that others should be afforded the same opportunity. As you begin to offer yourself unconditional love and acceptance, you will find these ideals rippling out into the world around you, having a wonderful, positive effect on all that you come into contact with.

When you begin to move toward self-actualization, settling into your skin and becoming your own best friend, there can be feelings of separation or not belonging. This may be amplified as you learn to **Hold Space** for others. Instead of rolling up your sleeves and slogging through life together, you come to realize that you are separate individuals, each on Her own journey. It's very important to not let your head tell you that this means you are unloved or unwanted or even misunderstood.

Instead, recognize this for the opportunity it is. The opportunity for self-nurture, for doing the things that make you feel content — to get a massage, sip a cup of hot tea while observing nature, read a book, or watch a movie you love. In my case, self-nurture usually involves a massage or energy work, and I love to go for a hike or sit in a hot tub. The other thing that really helps me to accept feelings of isolation, whether self-imposed or not, is to launch into an "attitude of gratitude." I have come to love and enjoy this time alone, rather than to resist it.

Before I come to the close of this book and send it out into the world to find you, I want to make sure that I am clear about something. I do not dislike the Alpha Female in me or in you. I respect her greatly. I recognize that the Alpha Female is an important part of who I have been and who I still am. I rely on her, and I trust her to step up to the plate when necessary and get stuff done. (Like writing this book.)

I also, however, have learned to respect the more vulnerable woman that I attacked in the mirror all those years ago. I didn't used to think there was any worth to Her. I told her flat-out, "You look like shit." If anything, she was a liability. But I now know the folly of that mode of thinking. This softer, more feminine, introspective aspect of myself is such a valuable and healthy part of me. It is she who will do the most important work; that of nurturing and accepting and fostering compassion.

The whole process has been incredibly liberating. I will likely spend the rest of my life working to truly embrace this new way of interacting with the world. It has taken a lot of work and a strong heart to stay committed to this transformation of self-acceptance. But, the freedom that comes with it is beyond description.

Balance is a tricky thing, whether in yoga, in health, or in identifying and pursuing your priorities. The same is true for balancing your inner life. The **Recovering Alpha Female** listens to the whispers of her heart and recognizes the valuable input of her intuition. The stronger she can become — the more "air time" she gets — the more the **RAF** can live a meaningful life while leaving behind the "need" to live up to everyone's standards but her own.

Becoming a **Recovering Alpha Female** is a process, and not an easy one, at that. It requires you to have huge faith, to turn your back on outmoded beliefs and cultural expectations in order to find something far more fulfilling. But, it is an empowering process that allows you to let go of what **They** say is right to instead pursue that which you know to be right for you. It allows you to stand in your own truth and to proudly be your own **you-nique**, graceful, feminine, quirky, wise, colorful self.

LEARN MORE ABOUT LINDY'S VISION!

LET YOUR COLOR OUT:

Supporting and inspiring over-achieving women to walk a little softer, appreciate the moment, and embrace their colorful quirks. **Let Your Color Out** is a for-profit company designed to inspire unconditional self-acceptance and **Hold Space** for transformation while empowering women to step fully into life, living colorfully and out loud.

www.letyourcolorout.com

UNDERGROUND KINDNESS:

A non-profit organization, presenting **Compassionists** into the classroom to introduce young people to the practice and philosophies of stress reduction and mindful living.

Underground Kindness creates a learning environment that is free of judgment, expectation and competition.

It is our vision to encourage and nurture the 'whole student,' through compassionate, all-inclusive classroom programs, such as: Anti-Bullying, Stress Management, Authentic Relating, Creative Journaling, Relationships 101, Yoga, Meditation, and Team Building, to name a few.

Our goal is to provide classes and workshops that support the growth of our teens into self-reflective, expressive, happy, healthy members of society. Students who are offered opportunities to relax, develop self-awareness and practice inter-personal skills, are more available for learning, are more willing to share their talents, and through compassion for self, are able to **ripple that back out into their world:** family, friends and community.

ALL UNDERGROUND KINDNESS CLASSES ARE FREE TO STUDENTS AND THE SCHOOLS!

We are supported 100% by the generosity of grants and donations.

KINDNESS IS CONTAGIOUS...

*For more information please visit
www.undergroundkindness.org

Printed in the United States
By Bookmasters